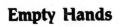

Empty Hands

Empty Hands

John D. Meehan

ST. PAUL EDITIONS

NIHIL OBSTAT:
  Rev. Richard V. Lawlor, S.J.
  Censor

IMPRIMATUR:
  ✠ Most Rev. Thomas V. Daily
    Administrator, Archdiocese of Boston

Library of Congress Cataloging in Publication Data

Meehan, John D.
    Empty hands.

    1. Consolation. 2. Peace of mind. I. Title.
BV4908.5.M37   1984   248.4'82   84-11379

ISBN 0-8198-2312-0
ISBN 0-8198-2313-9 (pbk.)

Cover credit: Rev. Gary Colton

Printed in U.S.A. by the Daughters of St. Paul
50 St. Paul's Ave., Boston, MA 02130

The Daughters of St. Paul are an international congregation
of women religious serving the Church with the communi-
cations media.

Table of Contents

Theme
Dedicatory Preface
Introduction
Part One—Images and Examples

Part Two—Directives

Theme

"A young person without joy and without hope is not a real young person."

(Pope John Paul II)

There is nothing that gives me certitude about my value as a person except my own free will. When I consent to the things which I deeply long for, I am full of joy and hope. And when I consent to the things that I do not want, I am full of sorrow and despair. It is, therefore, my own power of consent, my free will, which determines the condition of my life as a human being.

Dedicatory Preface

This very unoriginal piece of writing is dedicated to the many people who suffer from inner turmoil, who sense deeply the interior struggle, and who, through no fault of their own, are left abandoned on the barren soil of their own existence. To you my heart reaches out in sincere friendship, ardently wishing for you true peace, and the real hope of happiness.

However, it is not without risk that you read this book. It demands courage and confidence. I think you are capable; I *know* you are worth it.

JDM

Introduction

"O God, you will not the death
of the sinner, but rather,
that he be converted and live."

I have been urged to put into writing the
essential steps which are required for a human soul
to depart from its own inner struggle and begin a
journey toward a life full of joy and hope. It is my
intent to help those, especially the young, who
desire to get out of their pit of existence and give real
meaning and direction to their personal life. Weak as
I am and sinner though I be, I wish to help those who
want to undertake so worthy an enterprise as conversion, *metanoia*—a change of life.

One should not anticipate any magic formula or
any new discovery. Each will see that this small
book is nothing but a blend of the best, the purpose
of which is to stimulate joy and hope through the
means of images, examples and directives.

Part One presents images and examples; Part
Two gives directives.

Finally, this little treatise is written because the landscape of modern culture bears witness to the fact that too many people are wandering aimlessly and that their life is without purpose.

I want to speak to you who are struggling with what seems to you an all-pervading darkness in your life.

PART ONE

IMAGES AND EXAMPLES

The Olive Branch

No person is yet a real person unless in the ultimate depth of his heart he is full of joy and full of hope.

If this is true, then why do you despair? Why are you sad? Why are you anxious, uncertain, impatient, and unwilling, so you say, to commit yourself to anybody or anything?

If I answered for you and said, "Because I am unique and nobody understands me!", would I be right? If I said, "Because I'm all boxed in with no way out!", would I be right? And, if I said, "Because every time I think I have everything together, my head on right, my world collapses around me!" would I be right?

Am I right?

If I am, read on; if I'm not, read on anyway.

3

The Trip

There are a number of things you don't want to hear. You don't want a lecture or a sermon; and, you certainly don't want to hear about the morality of booze, drugs, sex, and rock music. Last, and certainly, you don't want any religious head games played.

So, let's start even, with the decks cleared: you and me, one-on-one.

Who do we start with: you or me?

Well, I'm easy and not very interesting. So, let's get me out of the way. I'm a know-nothing city kid who never did much of anything or accomplished much of anything, but am full of joy and full of hope.

Who are you?

Your name is _____. This means you're somebody. You know—you have parents, live in or at some pad, gobble junkfood, and have few or lots of friends. But is this your real I.D. card? I mean, is this who you really are?

How far back can you remember? Ten years? Seven? Five? Three?

I remember you very well, long before that. You came from a home where no one knew what you would look like, sound like, think like, or laugh like. You don't remember that home or how you started there or even got there. Under your mother's beating heart, you began your life in her womb and, from that day forward, you headed for the tomb. Life and death at the same time.

Funny, huh?

Each day you got bigger and, one day, you busted loose, sucking into your lungs that first rush of fresh air, and let out, for the first time, that special voice that identified you as you; the you that everyone was waiting for. Cut from the umbilical cord, you were set free and, now, were on your own.

Time passed: pabulum, strained carrots, cut-up hamburger, and ice cream; diapers to denims; birthdays and the beach; tonka toys to two-wheelers; Sesame Street and Star Wars; backyards for barbecues; sports is life.

What a life!

Crash!

One day you woke up and everything dissolved: funny-looking parents, weirdo friends, a pretty ugly face in the mirror, a changing body out of control, a messed-up mind and nowhere to go, no one to turn to.

"Try it, baby, it takes away the pain. Adults not only don't know, man, they really don't care."

And so, you slid. Down. Down. Down. Laughing! Crying! You put on the front with your friends;

you cried on your pillow at night—*alone*. You broke down inside: "Why me? I didn't ask for this; I don't want this!"

"Get a job!"

"Get a degree!"

"Get ahead!"

"Run, baby, run, or you'll finish last!"

"MAN, YOU AREN'T EVEN IN THE RACE!"

The tomb looms straight ahead and it's down. You've been down so long that it's beginning to look like up.

"Rocky"

"Chariots of Fire"

"Head for the Mountain"

It's the Pepsi generation, man, there ain't nobody but you.

"Take a snort because this coke's the real thing."

The College of my choice: Party U., a "rack" a day, three D's and an Incomplete; Fort Lauderdale, Aspen and the Cape. Big Sur's commercial; the Beach Boys sold out.

Real Rock: Metal! Metal! Metal! That's what's in; so is herpes.

Join the service (where's El Salvador?): three square meals, a regular paycheck, and start all over again. The Black Wall with those names on it say, "Don't do it." The flag is on my seat; the nukes are at my heart. The world according to Vonnegut; he eats quiche.

Forty hours on some assembly line; it's a cage. Fridays are Mondays; Wednesday is death. No raise; you're fired; do not apply: you do not qualify. Unemployment is 10%; what's my percent?

Listen, brother, you need a three-piece suit, an MBA, and to be "born again": haircuts are necessary. Listen, sister, you need a three-piece suit, an MBA, and to compete again: haircuts are necessary.

The Dallas Cowboys played the New York Yankees in Disneyland for the Burger Kingship! Sponsored by B.O. plenty.

"You Needed Me"—"Where Are the Clowns?" What's your song?

I'm wasted, conked out, and 21.

* * * * *

This is your captain speaking: our plane has landed; the trip is over.

* * * * *

The Triangle

Unto me, my faithful child,
confide your trip and weary trial
rest in labor, coolness sweet
tempering the burning heat
sweet refreshment, sweet repose
truest comfort of my woes
(Some Poet)

It's over. Sit back and relax. And please, don't worry. You ARE unique, but not in the way you think. Your SAT's don't count here: you do.

What happened to those happy days of youth? What happened so quickly that it made a fast food chain look like an unemployment line?

Really nothing; really something.

First, the nothing.

Every young person has to grow up. It's natural; it's good. The problem is you thought there was only one umbilical cord: the biological one. Everyone has a belly-button: the scar that certifies your birth into humanity as a person. A nine-month wait to enter the world, the "real world." The water broke and human hands extended themselves to receive you, cleaned the mess that surrounded you, and kissed your forehead as a sign that you were wanted and loved.

Beautiful! All the *joy* and all the *hope* for you from those around you.

But!

No one told you about the second umbilical cord, the scar it leaves, the mess that's left, the hands that aren't there: *no* joy, *no* hope.

Did they? Did they!

Let's call the second umbilical cord the triangle cord.

This cord is invisible and it's inside. You can't see it, but as you grow, you feel its pull, you sense its pain. It pulls you into yourself, away from others, and toward the unknown.

Visualize a triangle. You have been pulled toward the apex, leaving the old world behind. The journey up has been strenuous, painful and lonely, but from the top the journey down looks scary, dark, and deadly. You fought your way out of the old world to find yourself, but now, like the law of gravity, you are being pulled down into the unknown. Something must connect these two worlds, the old and the unknown—but what? Inside you are torn, a world split apart.

How did this happen? Who did it? Why?

How?

It just happens because you're human and you have to grow up, just as the sun must come up, just as you had to come out of the womb. The difference in the triangle cord is that there is no one to receive you outside of yourself. You're all alone in this new birth.

Who?

You! You did it because you wanted to grow up. You kept asserting yourself, your individuality, your uniqueness, your freedom. You even said to yourself at one point: "I gotta be me."

Why?

Because you have to be you; you can't be someone else.

So, there is nothing wrong with you; you're normal.

What went wrong then: why no joy; why no hope?

There's no joy because you don't know yourself well enough; and how can you take joy in someone you don't know?

There's no hope because you don't know where you're supposed to be going and how it is that you're supposed to get there.

Remember the triangle? It's not what you are or what you're doing that's going to let you slide down into the unknown of life; it's who you are that will let you dive, *joyfully* and *hopefully,* into that unknown. It's not death, it's life. It's not murder; it's joy. It's not suicide; it's hope. And, the real bottom line, the base leg between the old world and the new world, the line between the two bottom points is LOVE.

Elmer Gantry asks: "And what is love?"

The Ego

In talking about other people, we often ask, "Why doesn't he recognize his own faults?" On the other hand, we who see the faults are sometimes revealing our own.

How could we say: "She is selfish," "She is vain," unless we already knew in our hearts what it meant to be selfish or vain?

Dr. Jekyll and Mr. Hyde—the story of every human born of woman (Note: You can't be born of man).

The ego is what we think we are.

The I is, in fact, who we are.

The ego is the spoiled child in us.

The I is our personality.

The lives of these two selves cannot be lived simultaneously. If we attempt to do so, we suffer remorse, anxiety and inner dissatisfaction.

If true freedom is to be found within ourselves, the ego must yield itself to the birth of our true personality.

Like a plaster cast, the false ego has to be cut away, pulled off, and this is a process that involves detachment, pain and some indignity.

When the ego dominates our lives, we blame our faults on others and excuse great offenses in ourselves.

We wrong others and deny any guilt; others wrong us and we say they should have known better.

We hate others and call it zeal; we flatter others for what they can do for us and call it love; we lie to them and call it tact.

We are slow to defend the rights of others in public and call it prudence; we push others aside and call it getting our just rights.

We judge others and say we are facing the facts; we refuse to give up our life of filth and call anyone who does so an escapist.

We overeat and undereat and call it health.

We pile up more wealth than is necessary and call it security; we resent the wealth of others and call ourselves defenders of the downtrodden.

We begin our sentence with "I" and condemn our neighbor as a bore for wanting to talk about himself when we want to talk about ourselves.

We believe we are virtuous simply because we have met someone who is vicious.

Our sloth and laziness we call living sensibly.

We want so much to be loved that we forget to love.

We nurse our own troubles so much that we fail to see the lovableness of others.

We possess money, plastic cards, and consume like pigs and think we have worth.

We criticize others unjustly with the excuse that they should know the truth about themselves.

We judge our virtues by the vices from which we abstain.

We refuse to make up our minds about anything and boast that we are broadminded.

We have horrors tormenting our own soul and love to hear of greater horror in others, or to see them on the screen or TV, in order that we may, for a moment, forget our own hell within.

This is the supremacy of ego over I!

The ego is the superficial self.

The I is the real self.

They are related like the husk to the seed.

The apple does not become a tree until the outer, covering pulp is shed and the seed is set free to grow.

The I is not revealed until the ego is removed.

* * * * *

"Upon the sighful branches of my mind
such is; what is to be?
the pulp is so bitter, how shall taste the rind?"
(Francis Thompson)

The Prophet

"Something which is almost incomprehensible to the human mind is America's fantastic greed for profit and gain, which goes beyond all reason, all limitations, all conscience."

* * * * *

"Now we hear the voices of Americans and in the West: give us the possibility to continue driving our beautiful cars on our splendid highways. Make it possible for us to play tennis and golf; let us mix our cocktails as we are accustomed to doing; let us see the beautiful, toothy smile in the glass on every advertisement page of a magazine."

* * * * *

"I have come to America. For two months I have been travelling the wide-open spaces. Here you do not feel the nearness of it all, the immediacy of it all, and here it is possible to miscalculate. Here you must make a spiritual effort to understand the situation."

* * * * *

"But let's take Vladimir Bukovsky as an example. He was told: 'Go away. Leave. Go to the West and shut up.' And this young man—a youth facing death—said: 'No, I won't go. I have written about the persons whom you have put in insane asylums. You release them and then I'll go West.' This is what I mean by firmness of spirit; to stand up against tanks."

* * * * *

"One cannot think only in the low level of political calculation. It is necessary to think also of what is noble, what is honest and what is honorable, not only on what is useful."

* * * * *

"In our heart and soul, we have to recognize that it's almost a joke now to talk in America and in the Twentieth Century about words like 'good' and 'evil.'"

* * * * *

"At the present time, this concept is widely accepted among lawyers—that law is higher than morality; law is something that is worked out and developed, whereas morality is something inchoate and amorphous. This is not the case."

* * * * *

Hungary; Czechoslovakia; Poland; East Berlin; AFGHANISTAN

* * * * *

THANK YOU FOR THE INTERVIEW, MISTER PROPHET.

WE DO INDEED SEEM TO LIVE IN *THE FIRST CIRCLE*.

HAVE YOU READ *THE GULAG ARCHIPELAGO?*

Albert Einstein: "The present problem is not that of atomic energy, but that of the human heart."

The Civil War

A shop in Detroit hung a sign with these words over its entrance: "Do unto others as though you were the others."

Few of us have much difficulty in seeking our own personal advantage. But it's something else again when it comes to showing the same consideration for the rights of others.

Abraham Lincoln was walking down the street with his two sons when the boys started quarreling.

"What's the trouble with your boys, Mr. Lincoln?" asked a passerby.

"The same thing that's wrong with the rest of the world," was Lincoln's reply. "I've got three walnuts and each boy wants two."

This incident reminds us that the bigger problems in the world have their roots in the selfishness of one person over another.

On the other hand, the world can be changed if a person puts love into a person who has none.

General Robert E. Lee and his army were suffering a severe defeat and, as he rode over to a quiet section of the battlefield, a wounded Northern soldier defiantly lifted his head and shouted: "Hurrah for the Union!"

The wounded soldier fully expected to be shot.

Instead, General Lee dismounted and replied simply: "I'm sorry that you are so gravely wounded. I hope you may be well soon."

"That spirit broke my heart," the soldier later said, "and I cried myself to sleep."

The love of people that made Lee a great leader was the same motivating force that was to bring out in Lincoln his extraordinary powers as a public servant.

The first Civil War: Cain killed Abel.

Love, then, is far more than a sentiment or an emotion. It is the spiritual force that each of us can bring to a fear-numbed world.

* * * * *

"Young ladies and gentlemen: it is not possible for everyone to have a great mind, but it is possible to have a great heart."

An alumnus who attended that graduation said many years later, "This is the only thing I remember from that day and many times when I felt hopelessly defeated, this has come back to me."

* * * * *

Charles Morgan: "There is no surprise more magical than the surprise of being loved."

"...With malice toward none and charity for all."

The People

Dr. Joseph Matarazzo, Psychology Department, University of Oregon:

"A good talk with a close friend can solve problems, or at least put them in perspective before they become overpowering. One of the problems we face today is a scarcity of friends."

Love...

Eddie Brown, a barber in Harlem, gives free haircuts to young kids one afternoon a week.

Every Monday from two to four o'clock, his shop is filled with boys age three to ten.

"I make my living off these kids," he explained. "I feel I owe them something."

Is Patient and Kind

Love...

Larry Cuozzo sells subway tokens in Boston. He says that his customers respond warmly to his greetings.

"People have their problems," he says, "but an early morning smile can't hurt them. In fact, I think it helps. I like my job, and part of the job is to try and make the passengers happy."

Is Not Jealous or Boastful

Love...

QUESTION TIME:

1. Do I refuse to budge when other ideas clash with my own?

2. Do I take out my frustrations on my family, schoolmates, or fellow workers?

3. Do I get so locked into my own concerns that I can't hear what others are saying?

4. Do I take pleasure in putting people down?

5. Do I take the heat when criticized?

Is Not Arrogant or Rude

Love...

Susan Martin, a mother from Iowa, reflected on her eleven years raising a retarded child:

"Those years have been fruitful. Our child took us out of our insulated world.... We broke out of those walls and saw the needs of other human beings."

Does Not Insist on Its Own Way

Love...

Max Hoffner, a contractor from Denver, decided not to sign a complaint against four teenage boys who were caught breaking into his office. Instead, he offered them jobs, feeling that more could be accomplished by helping them redirect their energies.

Is Not Irritable or Resentful

Love...

Marylynn McCulloch, a novelist from Oklahoma, suffered three strokes which paralyzed her left side before she was thirty. Discouraged, she imagined she would never write again. But gradually, a page a day, she resumed her work.

The pain intensified as she went on. Her husband committed suicide, and illness made her a cripple.

In a rare mention of her troubles, she said: "Sometimes I think God got me mixed up with Job. But Job never cursed God, and neither have I. I carry on."

Does Not Rejoice at Wrong, But Rejoices in the Right.

Love...

Jose Garcia, a sculptor from New Mexico, fashions statues out of the parts of old and used mechanical parts. He fashions artifacts from cast-off materials.

Bears All Things

Love...

Vinoba Bhave, a tireless man from India, walks about his country convincing wealthy landowners to give some of their property to impoverished farmers.

"He has proved beyond a doubt," said a countryman, "that love can overcome lust for wealth and that moral commitment can be employed to persuade the rich to share their riches with the poor. ...He is proving that the greatest social changes can be worked by love and not by violence."

Believes All Things

Love...

Claude Rougald, a Canadian hunting guide, dropped everything to drive a Cleveland man 1,000 miles to the deathbed of his father. Leaving his family, he drove the man home and refused payment for his services.

"I've never met a more wonderful man. If there were more people with his sense of humanity, we would have none of the problems we have today."

Hopes All Things

Love...

An eager group of college students called on the city hall of Bigtown, U.S.A., and asked an official what they could do to help solve the problems of the cities.

His answer was blunt, but penetrating.

"If you're really serious, go back to your campuses and bury your heads in your books. Then, after you've got the skills to back your enthusiasm, come back and give the people of this city 20 or 30 years of your life."

Endures All Things

Love...

"THE HEART THAT LOVES IS ALWAYS YOUNG," runs the old Greek proverb.

Never Ends

The Press

HEADLINE: Perils of Pauline

SUB-HEADLINE: New sect, torn by divisions, gets novel plea for unity.

LEAD: (CORINTH)—A little-noticed religious movement is beginning to arouse interest and concern in this Greek metropolis of 60,000.

Adherents of this sect, known as "The Way," trace their origin to a Galilean carpenter, Jesus of Nazareth, who was crucified nearly three decades ago by Roman authorities.

NEWS ANALYSIS: The new religion arrived in Greece six years ago, brought by Paul of Tarsus, a tentmaker and itinerant preacher.

STORY: A novel feature of this fast-growing, underground movement is its insistence on "charity," a quality of mind and heart that wishes the good of others without seeking anything in return. It is associated with the attitude of Jesus who, it is said, willingly died for the good of all humanity. His followers assert that this Jesus rose from the dead and now exerts a powerful influence on them.

Dissensions, however, have threatened to splinter members of The Way, composed here in Corinth mainly of bronze workers, potters, shopkeepers and dock hands.

In an open letter from Ephesus to his co-religionists, the tentmaker Paul recently made an impassioned appeal for unity. In phrases verging on lyric poetry, he spelled out the significance of "charity" for those who practice "The Way" amid a population largely indifferent or hostile to their beliefs.

In words that are being repeated at corner marketplaces, slave headquarters and even some noble households, Paul stated the excellence of "charity" over many time-honored religious practices.

Informed sources have praised the rough eloquence of this letter. But they have expressed skepticism about its relevance or practicality in a city in which moneymaking, intellectual achievement, prostitution, slavery and ambition are such dominant values.

Whether or not Paul's words will heal the division of his sect and enable it to make further inroads into the traditional lifestyle of the Corinthians remains in doubt.

In the final analysis, the followers of "The Way" may be judged by the words of their Founder, Jesus of Nazareth: "By their fruits you will know them."

The Teenager

Q. "I can't take it any more."

A. If all the misfortunes of this world were laid in one big pile and everyone had to take an equal portion, most people would be happy to take back their own and leave, pronto.

Q. "My life is so empty."

A. People who complain about the emptiness of their life fail to realize that they're thinking too much about their own "inner vacuum" ("picking over the raw bones of their own psyche") and don't consider enough their own assets and direct them toward people who stand in need of the very abilities they have.

Q. "Nothing I do makes a bit of difference."

A. The world is full of human want. We must take our eyes off ourselves to see it. You don't have to look very far to find someone for whom your actions can make a big difference.

Q. "I haven't got what it takes."

A. Twelve years ago, a young man was playing with improperly mixed chemicals; they exploded. He lost his sight and both hands. This blind man with no hands serves as a rehabilitation counselor for the mentally ill.

Q. "If I could only get away from it all."

A. Do you know of any banks that give mortgage money to build a house on the moon? As long as we're on this planet our work is this: accept responsibility and bring some love into very earthly matters.

Q. "Nobody cares about me."

A. Bill Sands, an ex-con, has given talks on "going straight" to prisoners up for parole. He puts it this way: "When you're finally free, help others who are in the same fix. Once you stop allowing resentment to distort your life, you can put past experience to work for others. You may even help them avoid the same mistakes you made."

Q. "I just can't keep up with everything."

A. Who can? When personal problems appear unmanageable, world events totally beyond comprehension, resist the temptation to pull back into a private world or even a fantasy world. Stay in the *real* world and revitalize your thinking.

Q. "What's the use of trying?"

A. A young girl touched an electrical wire with her hand immersed in water. The policeman who arrived to help saw she wasn't breathing and had no pulse. He gave her "mouth-to-mouth," keeping at it until she showed signs of life. To try when there is little hope is to risk failure; not to try is to guarantee it.

Q. "You can't beat the system."

A. Anger or dissatisfaction with the system will never change it. Doing something will. Once you put your excuses aside, you can move ahead. A small candle of purposeful action is, in its own way, greater than all the darkness.

Q. "People are no 'blankety-blank' good."

A. A teacher looking at her new class and the roll book saw these numbers after their names: 138, 140, 145, etc. She said, "What a class, look at those I.Q.'s." The elated teacher tried new methods and the class responded exceptionally well to her creative approach. Later, she found out that the figures stood for locker numbers, not I.Q.'s. People will be as positive or negative as you expect them to be.

The Woman

Sally Ride
Althea Gibson
Amelia Earhart
Florence Nightingale
Susan B. Anthony
Mary
Pavlova
Marie Curie
Mahalia Jackson
Sandra O'Connor

"Since women are becoming ever more conscious of their human dignity, they will not tolerate being treated as mere material instruments, but demand rights befitting a human person both in domestic and in public life." (Pope John XXIII)

"I think we're involved in a whole identity search, both male and female. And because of it I think we'll all become better human beings."

(College Student)

"I realize now that all through high school and college, women competed with each other for a man. In our frenzy to become involved and attached, we distrusted each other and seldom stopped to form a human relationship with each other."

(Social Worker)

"A woman's role is to nurture, to give the warmth and care that makes living things grow, and every fulfilled woman I know, whether she's married or single, with or without children, does this."

(Publicist)

"Choose a business or a professional career; choose a life in the home; choose both, but choose whatever realistically lies within the limit of your potential. But first and foremost, *choose to be you*."

(Writer)

"A woman must seek her own affirmation of herself; she must like herself and what she is before she can love others for what they are. Of all confrontations, self-confrontation is the most difficult."

(College President)

The Man

"There is only one way in which one can endure man's inhumanity to man and that is to try in one's own life to exemplify man's humanity to man."   (Alan Paton)

(Mississippi)

A friendly passerby put this question to a tattered, whiskered man sitting on the steps of a tumble-down shack:

"How's your cotton crop coming along?"

"Ain't got none," was the response. "Didn't do any planting...afraid of boll weevils."

"Well, how about your corn?"

"Didn't plant any," came the response. "Afraid there wouldn't be enough rain."

"How about your potatoes?"

"Ain't got none. Scared of potato bugs."

"What on earth do you plant?"

"Didn't plant nothing," the man said with a yawn. "I just play it safe."

(New York)

Being held prisoner in his office for 25 hours during the campus rebellion of 1968 didn't dampen the spirits of Dean Henry Coleman of Columbia University.

"I'm delighted to say something positive about today's youth," he said on a television program.

(Idaho)

An old man sat rocking on his porch one spring night with his wife of 50 years beside him.

As if by sudden inspiration, he blurted out to her: "Sometimes when I think what you have meant to me all these years, it's all I can do to keep from telling you."

(Ohio)

Champion golfer Jack Nicklaus has won many tournaments not only by skillful playing, but also by carefully analyzing and correcting his mistakes.

During one championship match, his chief problem was faulty putting. So, he watched films taken earlier in the day in which he and his competitors appeared.

He immediately recognized the trouble: "I had been leaning over too far."

Before resuming play the next day, he practiced over and over on the putting green until he overcame his weakness.

He won the championship.

(Ireland)

> The New Left knows
> what the right hand
> holds
> in its palm.
> shades of the French
> Revolution;
> remember Robespierre.
> O do not tear all
> down, dissenters.
> build it up.
> encourage change and do
> not warn destruction's havoc for those unborn.
> in storming the
> ramparts of evil
> kill not the citizens.

(Colum Murphy)

(Germany)

When Ludwig Von Beethoven became deaf, he said, "What a sorrowful life I must lead"; then rising above the first defeat, he said, "I will seize the facts by the throat," and wrote great music he could never hear.

(Everywhere)

When men are ruled by fear, they strive to prevent the very changes that will abate it. Fear of change is, no doubt, in all of us. But it most afflicts the man who fears that any change will lead to a loss. When this fear becomes inordinate, he will abrogate the rights of others and the rule of law, using the argument that he does so to preserve them.

"...That there is no fear in love, but that perfect love casts out fear..."

The Child

If you want better people to make a better world, then you have to begin where people are formed and shaped—the family.

If a child lives with criticism,
  He learns to condemn;
If a child lives with hostility,
  He learns to fight;
If a child lives with ridicule,
  He learns to be shy;
If a child lives with shame,
  He learns to feel guilty;
If a child lives with tolerance,
  He learns to be patient;
If a child lives with encouragement,
  He learns confidence;
If a child lives with praise,
  He learns to appreciate;
If a child lives with fairness,
  He learns justice;

If a child lives with security,
  He learns to have faith;
If a child lives with approval,
  He learns to like himself;
If a child lives with friendship,
  He learns to find love.

(D.L.N.)

* * * * *

IF A CHILD LIVES WITHOUT A FAMILY, HE DOESN'T LIVE OR LOVE.

* * * * *

The greatest challenge facing parents today is teaching their children to think and act for themselves.

In his book, *What Shall We Tell the Children?*, Dr. Bennett Olshoker states:

"We should remember that our greatest gift to our children is to give them the ability to stand on their own two feet so that they no longer need us."

Parents have the task of forming children into mature and stable people. If they don't, someone else will form or deform them.

Only people carry the values absorbed in the home to the world outside.

Only people can give life and meaning to the words "respect" and "love."

Only people can listen attentively and sympathetically to other people.

Only people can assist the lonely, the oppressed, and the defenseless.

The future of all such values rests upon whether or not parents shape today's children. Because—

children are people.

The Home

"The world could be transformed in one generation, if all parents would practice what we now know about raising children ...there will be an unlimited future for mankind when this begins to happen."

(Dr. Charles Wahl)

Statistics (1983)

1. 79% of the men in America who have divorced, separated or plain "ole" left their families do not support them.

2. 25% of all children in America are living in one-parent families.

* * * * *

The home is intended by its very nature as an institution to be the primary source of inspiration and strength for parents and children alike. It is also intended to be the dynamic center from which they (parents and children) bring continually into the mainstream of modern life the human, moral, and spiritual values so essential as we enter the 21st century.

A 39-year-old author, who was only 10 when his father died, paid tribute to his parent in 1966:

"He left me with the notion that I had been put into the world for some purpose, and that the main business of my life was to find that purpose and do something about it."

Fathers and mothers are in a unique position. Others can assist them, but nobody can ever replace them fully.

Young people inwardly yearn for parental unity and firmness, even in their most rebellious moments.

"During this emotional riptide," says one expert, "your child wants you to stand like a rock."

Then, he added, "He or she wants to struggle against you, but they do so with the secret prayer that you will not yield. They are not rejecting parental values, they are testing them."

This "testing" may be severe:

* growing disinterest in school, poor attendance, indifference to achievement

* questionable companions

* lack of respect for the rights or property of others

* scrapes with the law, thievery, reckless driving

* most important—lying.

Don't hug your kid today—love him or her by finding out what they're doing and how they're doing.

A doctor warns: "As soon as your children leave the front doorsteps, they are catapulted into the tensions, temptations and cross-currents of our modern day."

Loren Eiseley in his book, *Adventures of the Mind,* stresses:

> A future worth contemplating will not be achieved solely by flights to the far side of the moon. It will not be found in space. It will be achieved, if it is achieved at all, only in our individual hearts.

* * * * *

Love of people should be such a dominant force in the home that it will be carried spontaneously into a world that may perish for lack of true love.

The Difference

"TWO MEN LOOKED OUT FROM PRISON BARS, ONE SAW MUD, THE OTHER SAW STARS."

Sally and Freddy got married. Fred's job was in the city. Sally and Freddy lived in the city. The apartment was home.

Freddy traveled a lot. You know: had to "move out" in order to "move up." Sally was alone most of the time.

Sally wrote to her mother and said she couldn't take it anymore and was coming home.

Mommy answered right away and replied with these lines:

Sally, you must learn to be sweet and gentle in all the events of life: in disappointment, in the thoughtlessness of others, in the insincerity of those you trusted, in the unfaithfulness of those upon whom you relied.

Learn to profit by the suffering that comes across your path. Use it so it mellows you, not hardens or embitters you.

May no one be less good for having come within your influence; no one less kind because they have been your friend.

Sally, love Freddy; don't come home, raise a family.

Love,
Mother

"SALLY AND MAMA LOOKED OUT FROM BARS, SALLY SAW MUD; MAMA SAW STARS."

The Natural Law

In D.C., a thief was arrested after holding up several stores in broad daylight. The police asked why he robbed during the daytime instead of at night.

"I'm afraid to be out on the street at night with all that money," he replied.

LAW I—THE LIAR MUST KNOW THE TRUTH BEFORE HE CAN TELL FALSEHOODS.

LAW II—THE THIEF STRIVES TO HAVE TRUSTWORTHY FRIENDS AROUND HIM.

LAW III—IMMORAL MEN PROTECT THE VIRTUE OF THEIR WIVES AND DAUGHTERS.

LAW IV—PERVERTS MASQUERADE AS THE OPPOSITE.

LAW V—ATHEISTS IN TROUBLE PRAY TO GOD.

LAW VI—PEOPLE WHO DENOUNCE MORAL-
ITY AS OLD FASHIONED WEAR A CLOAK OF
RESPECTABILITY.

LAW VII—CHEATS FEAR THEY WILL BE EX-
POSED.

LAW VIII—RAPE IS COMMITTED IN THE
DARK.

LAW IX—PEOPLE WHO "LIVE TOGETHER"
FORFEIT PEACE OF MIND AND HEART.

LAW X—"ONLY WHEN THE GOSPEL HAS
PENETRATED TO THE VERY DEPTH OF HUMAN
EXISTENCE WILL NATURAL LAW APPEAR IN ITS
FLOWER AND PERFECTION" (Jacques Maritain).

Shakespeare's *Richard III* (Act 1, Sc. 4) pays
tribute to conscience when he says:

A man cannot steal, but it accurses him; he
cannot swear, but it checks him; he cannot lie
with his neighbor's wife, but it detects him: 'tis a
blushing shamefast spirit that mutinies in a
man's bosom.

When people "mess themselves up," they are
dissatisfied. This is a hopeful sign in itself—a
persistent reminder that true serenity can be found
only in fulfilling a plan for a well-balanced life.

The Yardstick

The King of Urundi gave his African subjects just before they gained independence in July, 1962, this message:

"No one helps a parasite. Some of you think that after independence there will no longer be any law and each of you can do what he wants, steal and pillage, without fear of punishment. Get rid of this idea. We will keep peace and order with greater vigilance than ever."

* * * * *

Wise men of every age have recognized that there is but a single yardstick by which to measure our relationship with our fellow man.

The world's great religions put it this way:

BUDDHISM: "Hurt not others in ways that
               you yourself would find hurtful."
               (Udanavarga, 5:18)

HINDUISM: "This is the sum of duty: Do
               naught unto others which would
               cause you pain if done to you."
               (Mahabharaia, 5:1517)

ISLAM: "No one of you is a believer until
               he desires for his brother that
               which he desires for himself."
               (Sunan)

JUDAISM: "What is hateful to you, do not to
               your fellowman. That is the entire
               law: all the rest is commentary."
               (Ialmud, "Shabbat," 31a)

CHRISTIANITY: "Whatsoever you wish that men
               would do to you, do so to them;
               for this is the law and the proph-
               ets."   (Mt. 7:12)

REMEMBER VINOBA BHAVE?
REMEMBER GHANDI?
REMEMBER CONFUCIUS?
REMEMBER SOCRATES?
REMEMBER FRANCIS OF ASSISI?

* * * * *

DO YOU KNOW MOTHER TERESA?

* * * * *

The Shadow

"Naked I wait thy love's uplifted stroke!
My harness piece by piece thou hast hewn
    from me,
And smitten me to my knee;
I am defenseless utterly."

(Thompson)

It is not necessary to know much in order to love
much.

So, you want to ask me to do something for
    someone?
Tell me his name.
I love generous hearts who somehow can come to
    forget themselves.
Speak sincerely to me then.
Do you need a particular favor?
Make a list; read it in my presence.
Tell me frankly that you are prone to anger, that you

love sensuality and pleasure, that you are proud,
lazy, negligent and unstable.

Ask me to come to the help of your efforts, many or
few, which you undertake to free yourself from
these faults.

Do not be ashamed, you are not alone or unique;
many suffer the same defects.

What can I do for you?

If only you knew how much I would like to help you.

Are you perhaps sad, or in bad humor?

Tell me.

Who wounded you?

Who has mistreated you?

Come close to my heart for a refreshing balsam.

Are you perhaps afraid?

Do you feel a sadness that tears your soul apart?

Throw yourself in my arms.

I am with you.

I am at your side.

I shall not abandon you for one moment.

Do you feel ignored by persons who loved you once
but now have forgotten you without cause?

I will bring them back to you.

And don't you have some joys?

Share it with me like a friend.

Tell me what consoled and gladdened your heart.

Did you have a happy surprise?

Have you seen grave doubts disappear?

Have you received good news?

Maybe you have overcome some difficulty?

Did you come out of a trying situation?

Say, "Thank you."

Gratitude brings forth new gifts.

Do you have any promises to make?
Speak to me honestly.
Are you going to renew your life?
Are you going to avoid those bad companions?
Will you stay away from that disturbing situation?
Will you be kind to that person who has offended
   you?
And now, return to your life. Do not forget this little
   conversation. Please come again tomorrow.

Part Two

DIRECTIVES

Empty Hands

"It is just this—to find myself at my death with empty hands—that gives me joy, for having nothing I shall receive everything from God."

(St. Therese's Act of Offering)

I may sound preachy or negative. I don't mean to do this. It is only my love for you that makes me talk so fast and with total abandon. I'm so excited about you that, sometimes, I come on too strong.

Now, what is the source of all my joys and all my sorrows, from my youth onward, but the consent to do or not to do what I most deeply choose to do?

What I choose is, sometimes, to do what pleases me; at other times, to do what is good.

I found out that I could not have both all the time because, for the most part, they oppose one another. For instance, I want to do my studies but I would rather watch TV. Or, I want to be nice to my family, but I would rather be with my friends. This constant tension inside of me grew and grew.

I loved my body and what my soul could do for it. Therefore, I wanted to love both. Consistently, I attempted to reconcile these two factors, so opposed, and to make them realize that they were not enemies, but rather fellow workers. I wanted them to rejoice in harmony so I could rejoice in and with them. However, I found that the more I persisted in reconciliation and satisfaction, the more intense became my fear and sadness; *no joy, no hope.* I abandoned the moral and spiritual life in the hope that the intensity of the conflict would die down. It did—to a degree, and for a time. But, lifelessness and guilt surrounded me, taking all my happiness away. So, while the intensity of the struggle faded, an emptiness and darkness engulfed my soul.

I tried to fill it with pointless, useless, and meaningless activities: "keep busy and keep the inner war quiet." Yet, an ever-present, detached, clear, and interior voice protested: "This is absurd," while all the action went on. This made me angry. I began to war with everyone and everything: physically, morally, spiritually, and intellectually. And what struck me most was the fact that I never lost. So, I felt that I was unusual, that this problem was peculiar to me because I was unique.

Unwittingly, I ran away to college to get a know-nothing degree, as if this would help. It was there that I discovered that *every* person partakes of this inner war, because I met Augustine, Paul, and Plato.

This is when I discovered that the universal message of Christ, His *Good News*, is not a mystery of a particular religious sect. It is a universal statement about the nature of man: *ME*. I found that this interior struggle breaks out in every person's soul and that every human being longs for its reconciliation. In stark reality, I found the results of the struggles and the yearnings for resolution on the faces and in the eyes of the people I met and knew. Finally, I understood why they were the way they were and why I was the way I was.

But, I found out also that a weak soul does not have the endurance to resist the struggle for very long. It grows heavy, gives in, and the contest ends. Further, a weak soul cannot fight by itself. This is the nub of it all. All of us—you and I—are weak. I attempted foolishly to overcome this struggle by myself in order to find true and lasting happiness.

But what I really found was misery, despondency, despair, alienation, lack of purpose and orientation, depression, senseless activity, wondering what it is all about, saying: "If this is what it is all about, forget it," loneliness, and a dull, lazy life that was devoid of any true meaning. In my disgust with myself and with my life, I looked to anyone or anything in order to find some answers.

Instinctively, though, I didn't want the truth. I didn't like to hear those who spoke the truth. That truth, I knew, meant that I had to stop what I was doing; I must be serious, and I must change. I loved to hear the untrue answers because, between those lies and my selfish actions, I could push the struggle to the back of my soul.

In summary, I was in a state of alienation and disorientation.

Listen to a Pope:

> It is hard to find words to describe how profound is the darkness in which they are engulfed and, what is most deplorable of all, how tranquilly they repose there.   (Pope Pius X)

To get out of this condition I had to get a new view of life, a basic understanding of "conversion of heart."

Conversion of heart meant changing my life by concentrating on the Person of Christ.

Pope John Paul II made it clear that Christ redeemed the whole person; the whole Christ is for all of me.

This is the Good News! That is why I am joyful and full of hope!

It was important for me to face the facts, no matter how difficult it was.

All of us are:

1. creatures of God who assume dignity and worth because we are made in His image and likeness, distinct from the rest of earthly creation;

2. sinners by "propagation" and have all the propensities for self-glorification and -gratification and will be judged by a just yet compassionate Christ who is rich in mercy;

3. redeemed by Christ's blood and through Baptism are restored to a higher state than at the first creation; are recipients of all the gifts and graces of an heir and child of God, thereby, acquiring by gift, an integrity and eminence that surpasses the angels and, certainly, the beasts;

4. responsible for our own lives insofar as we are free to cooperate with grace or not, and for the lives of our neighbor insofar as the law of charity imposes upon us a charge to evangelize in the name of Christ;

5. called to perfection, sanctity and eternal happiness as a final end to our actions; and that call includes pain, suffering and poverty as constituent elements of this passage to eternal bliss;

6. placed in this temporal and passing order as the means to our sanctification and that labor is an essential instrument for attaining that end; and,

7. living members of Christ's Bride, Holy Mother Church, the consequence of which is an appreciation of the benefit of a divine Magisterium to which we freely submit and an attitude of docility where obedience is concerned.

This is the big picture, the "Catholic" vision, with all its human realities and in the Light of Christ.

I found out that He is the One Supreme Answer for me because He is the Word of God Who questions me, Who speaks to me with the words of Eternal Life, and Who finally shows me my grandeur, my duties, and my responsibilities.

Then, I looked at the real Jesus Christ:

His state was divine, yet He did not cling to His equality with God but emptied Himself to assume the condition of a slave, and became as men are; and being as all men are, He was humbler yet, even to accepting death, death on a cross. But God raised Him high and gave Him the name which is above all other names so that all beings in the heavens, on earth, and in the underworld should bend the knee at the name of Jesus and that every tongue should acclaim Jesus Christ as Lord to the glory of God the Father (cf. Phil. 2:6-11)

I saw that Christ embodied this love for me by "emptying himself." He did this not for Himself but for me. He loves me so much, that He gave His life upon the Cross for me: His "friend."

The bottom line, then, is love, *true love*: "He loved us first" (1 Jn. 4:10).

As I realized that Christ loved me first, it was clear that love was the one activity which I could not live without, because Divine Love allowed me to participate more intimately, more fully, and more continuously in the fullness of my personal life.

Now, a kind of horror always entered into my soul when love was demanded of me. Love in the abstract was praiseworthy; true love in my heart was traumatic. However, this fear did not discourage me. I kept two things firmly in mind. First, there was a way: "You shall learn the truth and the truth shall make you free" (Jn. 8:32). Second, there was help for me from Christ *personally*: "My grace is enough for you: My power works at its best in your weakness" (2 Cor. 12:9).

It is true that I write now of love while still being selfish. But it is not because I do not desire to love; it is my very desire and affection for love which encourages me to speak this way. As St. Augustine says: "It often happens that the office of distributing gives us the merit of receiving." So, it is my hope that while I try to point out the Way to you, God will impregnate my soul more deeply with His Love.

I stand before Him with "empty hands."

The War

"You were darkness once, but now you are light in the Lord; be like children of light, for the effects of the light are seen in complete goodness and right living and truth. Try to discover what the Lord wants of you, having nothing to do with the futile works of darkness but exposing them by contrast."

(Eph. 5:8-12)

The truth about conversion is easy; the act of conversion is not so easy.

This is a treatise on action. Very little will be said about principle. So, let me discuss the truth quickly.

Suffice it to be understood that sin is what is inherent in *every* person from birth and this condition comes from being born a human being; it is by propagation. This is the legacy of Lucifer and Adam. This is our nature. Thus, sin must be subdued in my life and love must rule it.

And, what is sin?

Sin is false love: a false love of myself.

It is a sense of superiority and a wish to shine above others. True love, on the other hand, is a sense of right place and a wish to excel with others which is the way God made us. What makes these two realities differ is the wish: Shine above place or excel within place. "Shine above" is wrong because it is out of place; it is out of place because it is a wish to be other than what we are: creatures. It is the desire to be a god or God Himself; to live our life without God.

It is not easy for us to identify the effects of Original Sin in any recognizable fashion because its roots are buried so deeply in our life, its vitality is so extreme, it springs up when we suppose it to be dead, it nourishes itself on so little, it is never satisfied, and it hides behind our personal worth and dignity. For the most part sin does not appear horrible to us: nothing is as deceptive as this fact. It disguises and transforms itself, it grows and spreads slowly. When it has finally taken possession of us, it is scarcely noticed; when it is noticed, it is excused. It appears less dangerous to us because it rarely assumes the form of a mortal sin as God's love intervenes constantly and persistently. He is a tremendous lover!

It is more correct to regard this condition as a deviation from the right love implanted in us by

God at Creation. This deviation assumes two forms: self-esteem and a desire for the esteem of others. These wonderful but wayward sentiments are deeply rooted in us. We will to love ourself and we will to be loved by others. The problem is not in loving ourself, but in loving ourself in place of, without, or above God. This false self-love has to be put back into its rightful place.

True love is self-love and its sentiments in order and in place. Thus, both the Old and New Testaments command us to love God and our neighbor *as we love ourselves.*

Because of Adam's fall and since Christ's total giving of Himself on the Cross for us, mercy is the new expression of God's love. The real aim of His mercy is to move us toward a favorable condition of true love and right happiness.

Pope John Paul II tells us:

The universal call to conversion fits precisely into this context. Since all are sinners, all need that radical change of spirit, mind and life that the Bible calls *metanoia,* conversion. And this attitude is created and fostered by the Word of God—the revelation of the Lord's Mercy.

Therefore, it is precisely because sin exists in the world—which "God so loved...that He gave His only Son"—that God, "Who is Love," cannot reveal Himself otherwise than as mercy.

Metanoia, conversion of heart, change of life, means and consists in discovering the Lord's mercy, i.e., in discovering that love which is "patient and kind" (1 Cor. 13:4). It means and consists in the basic prayer of David:

> Have mercy on me, O God,
> in your goodness.
> In your great tenderness
> wipe away my faults,
> wash me clean of my guilt,
> purify me from my sin.
> (Ps. 50:1-4)

King David, the sinner, in his plea reveals two key elements to us for changing our lives:

1. *the reality of sin:* "purify me from my sin"; and

2. *the psychology of reconciliation:* "wash me of my guilt."

Psychoanalyst Erich Fromm, who is not a Catholic, judges that the Catholic Church has "more adequate means" for dealing with sin and the sense of guilt. The "means" rest in the Sacrament of Penance.

A Church document on Penance released on February 17, 1983, states:

> It appears evident that the worthy celebration of the Sacrament of Reconciliation, and in its sphere, individual confession with the minister of Christ and the Church, responds to the deep psychological needs of man and can contribute to maturity and serenity of souls and to interpersonal relationships.

It then goes on to warn:

Some, having abandoned the celebration of penitence with individual confession, have begun to manifest the anxieties of their souls, and sometimes its guilts, to psychologists and with too much gullibility even to astrologists and others.

This shows clearly that left to ourselves, we tend to develop idiosyncrasies in moral judgment. Rationalization and denial of any self-evaluation easily take over our life when there is no personal examination of our conscience, no instrument for our purgation and God's forgiveness, and no access for atonement and reparation. Thus, Divine wisdom and love are manifested as mercy in the Sacrament of Penance.

Finally, we find out that the word "penance" comes from a Latin root which means conversion or change of heart. It recalls the message of Christ's first sermon, "Reform your lives and believe in the Good News" (Mk. 1:14). The phrase "Sacrament of Penance" reminds us that a reform of or change in our heart is absolutely indispensable to the forgiveness of sins and the washing away of guilt. The word "reconciliation" emphasizes that this Sacrament seeks to heal our relationships with God, others, and ourself which have been bruised or broken by false love: selfishness.

Pope Pius XII, in his encyclical *Mystici Corporis* (no. 88), confirms the integral role which the Sacrament of Penance should play in our life:

> But to ensure more rapid progress day by day in the path of virtue, we will that the pious practice of frequent confession, which was introduced into the Church by the inspiration of the Holy Spirit, should be earnestly advocated. By it genuine self-knowledge is increased, Christian humility grows, bad habits are corrected, spiritual neglect and tepidity are resisted, the conscience is purified, the will strengthened, a salutary self-control is attained, and grace is increased in virtue of the Sacrament itself.

The Sacrament of Penance and its regular use assists us in avoiding excessive or neurotic guilt or the extreme of letting ourself off too easily.

The mystery of God's mercy, concretely revealed in the Sacrament of Penance, becomes the source of a life different from the life which can be built by us alone, who are plagued always by the oppressive forces of threefold concupiscence (1 Jn. 2:16). This real condition is made worse by a life lived in the wasteland of this Modern Age.

> The dichotomy affecting the modern world is, in fact, a symptom of the deeper dichotomy that is in man himself. He is the meeting point

of many conflicting forces. In his condition as created being he is subject to a thousand shortcomings, but feels untrammeled in his inclinations and destined for a higher form of life. Torn by a welter of anxieties, he is compelled to choose between them and repudiate some among them—worse still, feeble and sinful as he is, he often does the very thing he hates and does not do what he wants (cf. Rom. 7:14ff.). And so he feels himself divided and the result is a host of discords in social life.

(Gaudium et Spes, no. 10)

Christ teaches us the mystery of mercy through one word: "forgive." Christ emphasized forgiveness so insistently that He gave Peter the immeasurable number "seventy times seven" (Mk. 18:22) when asked how many times he should forgive.

Pope John Paul II affirmed the heart of God's mercy through forgiveness by declaring in *Dives in Misericordia* that the whole of conversion can be summed up in the parable of the Prodigal Son:

The parable of the Prodigal Son expresses in a simple but profound way the reality of conversion. Conversion is the most concrete expression of the working of love and of the presence of mercy in the human world. The true and proper meaning of mercy does not consist only in looking, however penetratingly and compassionately, at moral, physical or material evil: mercy is manifested in its true and proper aspect when it restores value, promotes and *draws good from all the forms of evil* existing in the world and in man.... The genuine face of mercy has to be ever revealed anew. In spite of the many prejudices, mercy seems particularly necessary for our times.

(*Dives in Misericordia*, no. 6)

We know now that we have to be imbued with the fact that no matter how unfaithful we are, no matter how much the reality of sin and the psychology of reconciliation inundate us, God the Father, as revealed through His Son, can and never will be unfaithful to His Fatherhood, His love, or His mercy, and that He is eternally conscious of the natural and supernatural worth, dignity and value of us, His children.

The two elements of the reality of sin and the psychology of reconciliation, even though both have been overpowered by the Mystery of Redemption, have to be dealt with in a positive and diligent manner.

This positive and diligent manner includes the complete reality of reparation both in the sense of repairing our relationship with God and neighbor and repairing our own interior life.

Fr. Donald Pfannenstiel:

I know that I am a sinner, but I also know that I'm not evil. I need God and His help in order to be what He has called me to be in this life. I am totally dependent upon God. To say that I don't need God, to get my own way instead of His, to keep my commandments instead of

His Ten Commandments, to make excuses for being disobedient—that is to be a sinner. To continue to live in this way ultimately leads a person to believe not that he needs God, but that God needs him!

Reparation, then, is a willing act by which I try to 'repair' for a past act of offending God. While there are many means of making reparation, we shall look briefly at only two, both of which are Sacraments: Penance and the Holy Eucharist.

One of the problems with the Sacrament of Penance today is that we don't really make proper use of the Sacrament. We simply recite our sins to the priest, receive absolution, and after a while it may seem to us that the Sacrament really makes no difference. We become indifferent to it.

I like to compare the Sacrament of Penance with looking into a mirror early in the morning. What happens? We see in that reflection a groggy-eyed, messy and sometimes ugly person. Then why do we look into the mirror? To see ugliness? No! We want to see what it is we must do to make ourselves look presentable—wash, comb, shave or put on cosmetics, etc. We see what changes we must make on our person in order to be what we wish to be.

In a sense, that ought to be the way we use Confession. But what we often do is simply 'look in the mirror, admit the ugliness' and really do very little about it.

Our Lady has asked for the First Saturdays of Reparation, which includes the Sacrament of Penance. If I would follow this program and use the Sacrament of Penance as just described month after month, there would be a change in me, in my life, and in my relationship with Jesus and Mary.

And that's where Eucharistic reparation really begins. As I realize my dependence upon God, I begin to sense more and more the special nature of the Blessed Sacrament. The Eucharistic Presence becomes more and more important, not only that I am next to It physically, but also that I am spiritually aware of the tremendous power of the 'hidden Jesus.'

The closer I come to the Eucharistic Jesus present in the Most Blessed Sacrament, the more I will realize my own unworthiness, my own need to 'repair' my sins of indifference and ingratitude. I will discover more and more how much I really depend upon my Lord for everything. Without Him, I am lost! Without Him, I can do nothing!

In summation, then, Christ was and is the definitive Incarnation of mercy, its living sign for us at all times and in every condition of our life.

The Incarnate Word heard and answered the prayer of the murderer and adulterer, David. Why shouldn't He hear ours?:

You know I was born guilty—
A sinner from the moment of conception.
Yet you love sincerity of heart.

Instill some joy and gladness in me;
Let the bones you have crushed rejoice again.
Hide your face from my sins,
Wipe out all my guilt.
God, create a clean heart in me;
Put into me a new and constant spirit.
Do not banish me from your presence.
Do not deprive me of your Holy Spirit.

Be my savior again, renew my joy.
Keep my spirit steady and willing,
And I shall teach transgressors the way to you;
And to you the sinners will return.

(Ps. 50:5-13)

We must be impressed by the perversity of false self-love, and attempt to induce and to sustain within our own life a firm resolve to rid ourself of it. However, we must be aware that this resolve, not backed by action, will not rid us of selfishness any more than vague, feeble, or exaggerated assertions would.

So, we have to go to the root of the matter—beneath the conventional phrases and opinions.

"Do not suppose that I have come to bring peace to the earth: it is not peace I have come to bring, but a sword" (Mt. 10:34-35).

IF WE ARE READY TO REGAIN TRUE LOVE, WE HAVE TO GO TO WAR. This means we must pick up the sword. ACTION—ACTION, this is the great secret, this is the imperative need. We have to establish within ourself a confident love of God's mercy, opposing in daily, ceaseless conflict the contrary tendency to love ourself out of order. As I cannot totally eradicate false love, or its inclinations, it not only becomes an *all-out* war but, a *life-long* war.

Understanding and conviction are the advance guard—they clear the way. But only the army of daily deeds can achieve the victory for us. By these and these alone, God's love and mercy can be firmly established within our heart and soul.

True Christian peace is found only within the violence of true Christian combat. Governed by a resolute heart which is inspired by God's mercy, our new life employs this strength in the all-out war against our terrible selfishness. The result is tranquillity and harmony because we are heading in the right direction.

MERCY GIVES ME JOY, LOVE INSPIRES ME TO HOPE, WAR BRINGS ME PEACE.

The Steps

"Before God and before Jesus Christ who is to be Judge of the living and the dead, I put this duty to you, in the name of His appearing and of His Kingdom; proclaim the message and, welcome or unwelcome, insist on it. Refute falsehood, correct error, call to obedience—but do all with patience and with the intention of teaching."

(2 Tm. 4:1-3)

The act of changing one's life involves five main steps:

1. simple desire
2. solid resolution
3. purification
4. exercise
5. retreat

A. Desire

St. Bede explains conversion—initially *AND* daily—this way: "Three miracles take place in the cures by Christ: the dumb man speaks, the blind man sees, the possessed man is delivered from the Devil. These three miracles are repeated daily in the conversion of a sinner: first, the Devil is expelled; then, he sees by the light of Faith; and lastly, he opens his lips to praise God."

Anybody who is unhappy or dissatisfied with himself and his life is a prime candidate for conversion. The beginning is a simple desire to be happy or to be a better person than one is presently. This simple desire must be converted into a solid resolution to do something about it.

B. Resolution

The act of converting simple desire to a solid resolution necessitates a guide.

"A faithful friend," says the Book of Ecclesiasticus, "is a strong defense; and he who has found him has found a treasure. A faithful friend is the medicine of life and immortality; and they that fear the Lord shall find him" (Sir. 6:14-16).

This treatise is to serve as a guide. It is *NOT*, however, a substitute for a confessor or spiritual director.

St. Louis gave this advice to his son: "Confess often; choose a good confessor, a wise man, who may safely teach you to do the things that shall be necessary for you."

Who shall find this man? "They that fear the Lord" is the answer of the Book of Wisdom. They that are firmly resolved to advance their simple desire is my answer. You must pray to God, with the greatest insistence, to furnish you with a confessor or spiritual director as He did for Tobias. This person must always be an angel to you. This means that you are *not* to look upon him or her as a mere human, i.e., do not place your confidence in human learning, but in the Word of God that is spoken or to which you are directed. It is God who is speaking to you through this person, putting in his heart and mouth whatever is necessary for your happiness. Therefore, you must pay as much attention as if an angel were to appear. Open your heart with all *sincerity* and *truthfulness,* speaking *clearly* and *explicitly* the state of your conscience—without fiction or exaggeration. This accomplishes two things: your good actions are examined, encouraged, and confirmed; your evil ones are corrected, directed, and remedied. Further, you will receive *right* comfort and consolation. Place great confidence in this person, but be united with him in reverence. Confide as a child does to his parents.

The Little Flower urges:

For this end, choose one among a thousand, for there are fewer than can be imagined who are capable of this office. He must be full of charity, knowledge, and prudence. If any one of these three qualities is wanting in him, there is danger. But, I say to you again: ask him of God. Having found him, bless God, remain constant, and seek no other, but proceed with sincerity, humility, and confidence, and you will make a most happy journey.

C. Purification

Now, as the good desire appears and is converted into a solid resolution, you must put your hand to the pruning knife, to remove from your life all dead and superfluous works. This is purification, which means getting rid of the "old self" in order to put on the "new self" (Christ) by forsaking sin, by purging your selfishness, and by cutting away every obstacle which prevents you from going to God with *joy* and *hope*. An operation is required in a diseased soul in order to restore it to good health. Purification is the operation; sin is the disease.

And please, do not look for instant cleansing like the miraculous and extraordinary order of grace given to St. Paul and St. Mary Magdalen.

(Be realistic: read *The Confessions* of Saint Augustine, Ryan translation.)

Ordinary purification takes place only little by little, by passing from one state to another with *hard work* and *patience*. Courage is essential, and courage is a virtue of the will.

At this point it is necessary to focus upon human sexuality because of the conditions in our times and the inherent power of false love.

Catholicism has its own proper perspective on human sexuality. The Church sees sex as part of God's creation, a reality which does not have the body alone as its object, but involves the entire human being, a reality which has a determining role in the way a person matures, both physically and morally. It has a determining role in the development of a person's likeness to God.

Teaching spiritual values in human sexuality is sharing with people how to be genuine and mature and not self-centered in love, respecting loved ones for who they are, not using them for selfish gratification or hurting them by initiating intimacies prematurely. It is a living effort to protect people from cheap, selfish, and irresponsible attitudes toward human sexuality. Hesitancy to teach clear human, moral and spiritual values betrays a fundamental disrespect for true personality, freedom, and autonomy from which people suffer eventually.

A concern is expressed at times that telling people what they may not do will appear negative and be resented. Of course, great tact must be used when dealing with people. The approach must be such that they realize that what is being said is being said out of love, as friends caution friends. It is necessary to make clear that these prohibitions are not arbitrary or whimsical. They should be directions based on reality and to ignore them generally leads to suffering and, in some cases, a lifelong mistake.

In the Catholic context, the virtue that governs formation in human sexuality and its attendant love is chastity.

Chastity means to chasten, to cleanse, or to purify. In the moral and spiritual orders, people chasten themselves by purifying their conduct of what is evil, even if it means mortification. In a restricted, yet universally accepted sense, chastity is the virtue which purifies a person's conduct of any misuse of the faculty of transmitting life, keeps sexual powers free from any sinful activity, and enriches the personality by self-mastery and self-dedication to God. This means a stable manner of behavior by which an individual moderates the faculty of transmitting life and the accompanying pleasure, be it physiological or psychological, and this moderation accords with God's law.

Therefore, this moderation does not mean rare use or abstinence as though from something evil or unworthy, for that would be Jansenistic. It does exclude unbridled enjoyment, for that is hedonism. The word moderation comes from *moderamen*, meaning a guiding agent, like the rudder of a ship. God has set a course for human sexual activity; chastity is the rudder which keeps all people on that course. God also provided the natural and supernatural aids required to do so; man's part is to learn them and moderate his or her conduct accordingly.

A key element of chastity is modesty. Clementine Lenta writes:

> An all-but-forgotten virtue these days is modesty—rarely mentioned, rarely promoted. Yet it is a very important virtue because modesty protects the virtue of chastity. The lack of modesty is a serious matter because very often it

causes temptations, sins and scandal. Immodesty is, therefore, displeasing to God, an offense for which He holds everyone accountable.

Unfortunately, the vast majority of women and girls do not realize the seriousness of their responsibility. They simply do not seem to realize the devastating effect that immodest fashions can have on the beholder, sometimes contributing to the occurrence of rape and other sexual crimes, even murder.

The truth of the matter is that even though 'everyone' is wearing too-tight, too-short dresses; low-cut necklines; dresses made of transparent or clinging materials; backless, strapless evening gowns; skimpy bathing suits; too-tight sweaters, jeans and slacks; too-short tennis and golf shorts, as well as bras which unduly emphasize the contours of the body; still the popularity of such fashions does not make these styles modest. Neither can it be pretended that immodesty is in the eyes of the beholder. Immodest fashions are immodest—period!

Numerous saints, popes, spiritual fathers and retreat masters have repeatedly tried to alert people to the responsibility of upholding modesty. They have also strongly recommended that parents, pastors and teachers fulfill their duty of enforcing standards of modesty among their charges.

Added to these admonitions is that of Our Lady of Fatima who, in 1920, told Jacinta Marto, one of the seers, that 'certain styles will be intro-

duced that will offend our Lord very much....
People who serve God should not follow fashions. The sins which cause most souls to go to
hell are the sins of the flesh.'

We now note that immodest fashions have
not only been introduced but are 'flooding' the
fashion world. Even boys and girls are now
wearing too-tight slacks and too-tight, too-short
shorts.

The need for modesty and for awareness
of responsibility is quite a problem. Immodesty has become so prevalent that it has even
invaded the sacredness of the House of God. In
some churches women and girls attending Mass
and even taking part in the Offertory procession
are wearing immodest fashions.

'But,' comes the protest, 'what's the difference? Everyone wears such styles. And besides,
God doesn't care about fashions as long as we
get to Mass.'

Doesn't He?

Isn't that actually our own opinion, rather
than His? Doesn't He expect us to follow His
commands regarding purity and modesty? And
didn't He voice a very strong condemnation of
scandal-givers? (cf. Mt. 18:16)

Added to the irreverence and the immo-
rality of immodesty are the physical dangers
involved. It is common knowledge today that
women and girls feel that they cannot safely
walk alone on city streets at night even in the
early evening. The statistics on sexual crimes

continue to climb. Ways and means of preventing such crimes are being investigated, but the one simple means which could be of tremendous help—the promotion of modesty—is being widely ignored.

'What,' we ask, 'can we do about promoting modesty?'

There are so many things which could be done. Naturally, any corrective measures must start with one's self and within the family circle before such efforts can extend into the community and ultimately into the world. First of all, you and I—men and women—must dress modestly at all times. Next, mothers and fathers must set a good example, must instill in their children an appreciation of the importance and the beauty of the virtue of modesty, and then see to it that their children practice modesty and purity.

Of course, sometimes we may have to shop around quite a bit, and we may have to settle for a different color or fabric from the kind which we wanted to buy. We may have to lengthen hems and/or make other alterations—a bother, of course—but it can be done. It should be done.

It is interesting to note that the late, holy stigmatist, Padre Pio, whose cause for beatification is underway, often deplored the prevalence of immodesty and repeatedly urged a return to modesty. He also said that a very special blessing will follow those who work towards bettering this condition. Sister Lucia, to whom

Our Lady appeared at Fatima, recently stated: 'When I think of the United States I think about this: one of the things which Our Lady especially asked for was modesty in dress. There does not seem to be much modesty in the life of the women of your country. But modesty would be a good sacrifice to offer Our Lady and it would please her if the Catholics in your country would make a league for modesty in dress....'

Effort and cooperation, backed by prayers, patience and perseverance, could turn the trend away from immodest styles to modest fashions. After all, the present immodest designs did not occur all at once. Apathy emboldened designers to create more and more immodest styles. It will naturally be difficult to stem and reverse the tide, but, with God's blessings, it can be done. It may be an uphill struggle but the start towards modesty must be made. As the old saying goes, 'the longest journey of a thousand miles begins with a single step.'

It is encouraging to note that there are still priests who are courageous enough to preach modesty and purity, still nuns who do not tolerate students wearing immodest fashions, still parents who give good example and who teach their children the value of modesty and purity, and still teens who want norms and discipline and a change in current fashions, literature and entertainment.

In fact, as one youth recently put it, bluntly and cogently: 'Just because the trade pushes immodest styles; just because many books, movies, TV programs and advertisements are more and more disgusting, do we have to take all that stuff? Do we have to be such fools?'

Well—do we?

So, immodesty demonstrates that we live in times when chastity is belittled and tragically discarded.

On September 13, 1972, Pope Paul VI, in forthright language, told us where widespread harm is done:

> ...on the scientific plane, psychoanalysis; on the pedagogical plane, sex education; on the literary plane, obligatory eroticism; on the advertising plane, base allurements; on the plane of entertainment, indecent exposure straining toward the obscene.

Chastity, then, touches upon the inmost and basic inclinations of human nature which means a call for personal maturity, proven by self-mastery over thought, imagination, emotion, appetite, and desire. It requires genuine personal charity towards God and our fellowman. Charity makes love between a man and a woman chaste; if it is absent it degenerates into lust. Charity, therefore, is a necessary factor in the full development of human dignity and maturity, the goal of every right-minded person.

As sexual maturity goes hand in hand with emotional maturity, education for chastity means, in large part, educating the heart. It is a problem of love. Human love is not perfect from the start; it must develop and become perfect through a long process of growth and purification. In young people, it can easily become sense-oriented, egoistic, and self-indulgent. But, as the young person becomes mature, this human love should become spiritual, unselfish, and self-sacrificing. In the process of this growth, care must be taken to avoid any type of compromise which falls short of the ideal we are looking to attain—living the life of Christ more fully.

This means that a person's own enormous reserves of affection and the powerful tendencies toward human sexual relationships must be developed and controlled.

Ideals ought to be emphasized—ideals of honesty, sincerity, goodness, generosity, self-giving, and heroism. People should be encouraged and helped to form *real* and *uplifting* friendships. At the same time, the sentimentality of immaturity has to be sobered, purified and regulated.

People must be aware that, despite the essential goodness of human sexuality and despite the fact that through the grace of redemption "the law of the spirit of life in Christ Jesus has set us free from the law of sin and death" (Rom. 8:12), the liberation which fits one to serve God in newness of life *does not* extinguish the concupiscence deriving from Original Sin or the promptings of evil in the world, particularly in this age when permissiveness and hedonism have resulted in the unrestrained exaltation and perversion of human sexuality, especially through the media of social communication and public entertainment.

All people have free will which means they are capable of accepting or rejecting, obeying or disobeying God's law. Morally, however, they are not at liberty to reject what God has enjoined; they are bound to exercise their free will by accepting His law.

Everyone should do everything possible to foster chaste and responsible conduct among people by encouraging:

* frequent reception of the Sacraments of Penance and Holy Eucharist;

* prayer, word, and example;

* good and healthy friendships;

* patient and practical advice;

* avoiding occasions to sin; and

* adherence to the teachings of the Catholic Church and the Holy See; they anchor chastity in the Eternal Law.

Is it any wonder that Christ pronounced the Beatitude: "Blessed are the clean of heart for they shall see God"?

He did not limit His words to one culture, one place, one people or one century. He addressed Himself to all men and women of all nations and of all ages. Though uttered at one moment of history, His Divine Rule permeates all of history.

Single-minded charity leads to clean-hearted chastity. Chastity concerns the whole personality, as regards both interior and exterior behavior: "Your body, you know, is the temple of the Holy Spirit who is in you" (1 Cor. 6:15).

Chastity, motivated by Divine Charity, makes people pure in body and clean in heart. If they persevere to the end, they shall see God.

D. Purification from Mortal Sin

In the Gospel of St. Matthew (12:22-32), we see the terrible tension between Satan and Christ over the soul of the possessed man. Christ casts out Satan. This is what we must do to our souls: by the power and grace of Christ cast out Satan, who is one but not the only author of mortal sin. This is done through the Sacrament of Penance. Seek the best confessor you can find to help you. The Laws of God and His Church constitute the rules for examination.* Prepare and collect (you may, but are not obliged to use paper if your memory is poor) your *knowing, willing* and *grievous* violations of these

---

* The laws of God and His Church are the following:
THE LAWS OF GOD:
1. I, the Lord am your God. You shall not have other gods besides me. 2. You shall not take the name of the Lord, your God, in vain. 3. Remember to keep holy the Lord's day. 4. Honor your father and your mother. 5. You shall not kill. 6. You shall not commit adultery. 7. You shall not steal. 8. You shall not bear false witness against your neighbor. 9. You shall not covet your neighbor's wife. 10. You shall not covet anything that belongs to your neighbor.
THE LAWS OF THE CHURCH:
1. To keep holy the day of the Lord's resurrection: to worship God by participating in Mass every Sunday and holy day of obligation: to avoid those activities that would hinder renewal of soul and body, e.g., needless work and business activities, etc. 2. To lead a sacramental life: to receive Holy Communion frequently and the Sacrament of Penance regularly—minimally, to receive the Sacrament of Penance at least once a year (annual confession is obligatory only if serious sin is involved);—minimally, to receive

Laws. All knowledgeable and willful violations in serious matters are grievous. Detest and renounce them with the greatest conviction, contrition and sorrow you can muster. This is essentially an act of intelligence and will. If you think about it earnestly enough, it may well overflow into *feelings* of contrition and sorrow. If so, that is a great good, but it is not necessary. To help you do this, keep in mind four things: 1) you have lost the grace of God; 2) you have given up your place in heaven; 3) you have chosen the *eternal* fires of Hell; 4) you have turned your back on Him who created you for life and redeemed you by His death. A good confession not only expels Satan and removes mortal sin, but it calms our hearts, composes our minds, opens us to spiritual advice, and gives our soul the confidence to accuse ourselves openly in succeeding confessions.

As this purification from mortal sin is really a call to renovate your life, I urge all "first-timers" to make a General Confession, if the confessor approves.

Holy Communion at least once a year, between the first Sunday of Lent and Trinity Sunday. For a good reason, the precept may be fulfilled at another time during the year. 3. To study Catholic teaching in preparation for the Sacrament of Confirmation, to be confirmed, and then to continue to study and advance the cause of Christ. 4. To observe the marriage laws of the Church: to give religious training (by example and word) to one's children; to use parish schools and religious education programs. 5. To strengthen and support the Church: one's own parish community and parish priests; the world-wide Church and the Holy Father. 6. To do penance, including abstaining from meat and fasting from food on the appointed days. 7. To join in the missionary spirit and apostolate of the Church.

E. Purification
from the Affection
for Sin

While most people will recognize their sins, will confess them, and will firmly resolve before God and to themselves not to sin again, they do so with a certain reluctance because of the loss of an apparent or real pleasure. These people are like the sick man who is told that alcohol will kill him. He quits drinking because the doctor has threatened him with death, but does so with the utmost reluctance. Such is the case with weak and lazy penitents. They abstain from sin for some time, but it is with regret. They would rejoice if they could sin and not go to Hell. They speak of sin like the child who pouts when telling his visiting grandparents how his parents won't let him go home with them. (The reason the parents don't let the child go is because of the impact an extended stay with "spoilers" will have on his already too-selfish disposition.) They speak of sin with some relish; they laugh with delight or snicker at past or recently witnessed sin. They act as if those who sin are at peace with themselves and they, the penitent, are the miserable one. You will hear them say, "Boy, it's a good thing I went to confession, or I would...," or "If it wasn't for the fear of Hell I would...." You see, they are purified from the state of mortal sin, but still have a strong affection for it. They are like the Israelites who leave Pharaoh's land for the Promised Land but, in the desert, long for the "flesh-pot" city of Egypt. These people are still in serious trouble and must be purified from the affection for sin.

This affection for sin not only affords the distinct possibility for a relapse into mortal sin, but weakens and depresses our spirits in such a way that it becomes almost impossible to perform good works promptly and with joy. These people are like the husband who gets the symptoms of "morning sickness" from his pregnant wife: he isn't sick, but all his actions are sick. They sleep without rest, eat without enjoyment, laugh without joy, drag themselves about, work without purpose or zest, physically turn pale, are short-tempered, and, in a nutshell, are people with whom we wish not to associate.

These souls may do good, but with such a spiritual heaviness that it takes away all the happiness from their good acts which, by the way, are often few in number and small in effect.

F. Purification from the Affection for the Useless

Music, play, dancing, feasting, partying, fine dress, drinking, golf, movies, television and theater shows considered in their substance are indifferent. They may be used well or ill. Nevertheless, these things are always potentially dangerous; and to have a strong affection for them can spell trouble. The evil does not consist in partaking of them, with moderation and the law considered, but in a fond attachment to them. They are affections which take up needless room in our heart and sap the sweetness of our soul. A heart that burdens itself with materialistic, unprofitable, superfluous, and dangerous affections certainly cannot run readily, lightly, and easily after its God, the true end of its love.

Children amuse themselves and run after butterflies. No one finds fault with them because they are children. But is it not ridiculous and absurd or, more pointedly, a sorry sight to see persons advanced in years fix their heart on worthless trifles as those which I named? It is from our dependence upon these things that we must be purified. Devotion and meditation, along with self-denial, help us.

G. Exercises

The spiritual exercises which sustain our souls, incline our will, habituate our deeds and facilitate our cooperation with grace are:

1. Mass
2. Sacraments
3. Bible
4. Rosary
5. Prayer
6. Acts

1. Mass

The greatest spiritual activity that a person can engage in on this earth is the Holy Sacrifice of the Mass because he comes in direct contact with the action of God and, more, with the grace of God, and more still, with God Himself. The Divine enters into the human. *Go to Mass every day of your life; never miss Mass if possible.* Present-day occupations and poor parish schedules make it difficult. However, there is rarely a solid reason why a person can't make it to Mass on a regular basis.

2. The Sacraments

Go to the Sacrament of Penance at least once a month.

Receive the Holy Eucharist every day. Unless in a state of mortal sin, never deprive yourself of the Body and Blood of Christ. You are never worthy enough to receive Him, so don't put false humility into your soul and deprive it of its sustenance. You don't use that kind of thinking for your body; don't use it for your soul.

3. Bible

Holy Scripture is the Word of God. It beckons and moves you to Him. Read something from the Bible every day. This holds true especially for beginners in prayer. Read for a short time; think about what you have read. Read at least fifteen minutes a day.

4. Rosary

The Fatima Message is clear.

It has been restated in very specific terms through appearances by Our Lady to a lay catechist in Nicaragua during 1980, authentically corroborated by His Excellency, the Most Reverend Pablo Antonio Vega, on November 13, 1982.

Our Lady's last message to Bernard Martinez, the catechist, on October 13, 1980, was:

'Pray the Rosary. Meditate on the mysteries. Listen to the Word of God spoken in them. Love one another. Love each other. Forgive each other. Make peace. Don't ask for peace without making peace; because if you don't make it, it does no good to ask for it. Fulfill your obligations. Put into practice the Word of God. Seek ways to please God. Serve your neighbor, as in that way you will please Him.'

Bernard told Our Lady that he had many requests for her and Our Lady said:

'They ask of me things that are unimportant. Ask for faith in order to have the strength so that each can carry his own cross. The sufferings of this world cannot be removed. Sufferings are the crosses which you must carry. That is the way life is. There are problems with the husband, with the wife, with the children, with brothers. Talk. Converse so that problems will be resolved in peace. Do not turn to violence. Never turn to violence. Pray for faith in order that you may have patience.'

Afterwards she added:

"You will no longer see me here."

Three times the catechist cried out: "Don't leave us, my Mother!"

She then spoke her last words:

'Do not be grieved. You will not see me here again, but I will be with you.'

And she told him to invoke her as "The Mother of all, the Mother of all sinners."

Bishop Vega, in publishing the accounts exactly as given by Bernard, noted:

For our part we are surprised at the emphasis given to the responsibilities that weigh on man and the duty to make peace and to construct the world. This is a religious emphasis not typical of popular piety, which tends to leave everything up to God.

So, pray the Rosary and meditate on the mysteries. This "sacrament" of the Blessed Mother arouses and sustains charity.

5. Prayer

There is nothing that purges your will of its evil inclinations more effectively than prayer because it is a personal act. The best form of prayer is mental prayer, i.e., conversing with God with your mind and heart. The best form of mental prayer is thinking about the life and words of Christ and how you fit into them. The best time for prayer is early in the morning, when the mind is less distracted and is refreshed after a night's sleep. For most people the maximum time for prayer is one hour at one sitting, no more. Working and active people should break the hour up into at least three twenty-minute periods during the day: morning, afternoon, and evening. The best place for prayer is in Church in the presence of the Blessed Sacrament. The best position for prayer is a posture that conforms to the dignity and reverence of the activity and assists you to converse with God. You will not, at all times, be able to accomplish *all* the *best,* but seek a combination which best approximates the object: talking *and* listening to God with heart and mind.

You will be required to engage in vocal prayer, e.g., at Mass, the Rosary, etc. You must fulfill your obligations. However, when you choose to say vocal prayers and find you are tending to drift toward mental prayer, do so. You will have made a higher choice. God is more pleased with the higher choice, so don't worry about finishing your vocal prayer. If your duties prevent you from saying vocal prayers or mental prayers and from going to Church, sanctify your duties by offering them to God in prayer, i.e., consistently keep in mind that what you are doing is being done in the service of God and, *always,* do your best. If your duties are such that they leave you really no time, or tend to make you forget to say your prayers, then when you can find time or when you remember, say your prayers *then.*

Begin all your prayers, whether mental or vocal, in the presence of God and ask His assistance to help you to pray. Abide by this rule, *without exception,* and you will see the profit in it.

By the presence of God I mean: 1. making your heart aware that there is The God and His Presence is real, no matter where you are; 2. arousing your heart to move toward Him because He is present; 3. consider Christ in His divinity: we are children who believe in Him and, therefore, can ask Him, in candor, about anything; 4. use your imagination to arouse your sense of His humanity. After you have put yourself in His presence by doing any one or a combination of 1-4, ask additional help from your Guardian Angel or Patron Saint so that they will lead you into the way of prayer.

After this preparation, propose to your soul what you intend to meditate upon. This proposal confines your meditation and keeps it from rambling to and fro. After meditating upon it try to understand it. After understanding it, consider earnestly how you can apply it to yourself and your life, for the purpose of bettering your life by helping others. Then, resolve and decide which points you can dwell on for the rest of the day or until your next prayer time.

Remember, actions meditated upon and contemplated about, but *NOT PRACTICED* tend to puff up your ego and encourage you to imagine that you already are what you have imagined yourself to be or resolved to be. This is especially true when your resolutions are lively and specific and not put into practice: the result is vanity and, therefore, danger. At all costs then you must strive to practice your resolution and to seek every occasion, however small or great, to do so. For instance, you can seek to act mildly toward those who offend you by meeting and greeting them kindly. If you should not meet them, at least you can speak well of them and pray to God on their behalf. After finishing your prayer, be careful not to disturb your heart by jumping too quickly into the action of the day. Ease your way in, in order to retain as much inner reflection as possible for as long as possible.

6. Acts

The first act of your day is to prepare yourself for all the acts of the day: 1. adore God and thank Him for preserving you through the night; 2. note that the day has been given to you as a means of gaining eternity and employ the day for that intention: *you want to go to Heaven;* 3. foresee the day and what situations you may encounter which can move you toward God and which will offend Him through selfishness or other irregularities; 4. prepare yourself for the day by resolving not to entertain any temptations; 5. acknowledge your inability to keep from falling on your own; 6. ask for the grace to get through the day. All this can be done briefly and fervently: before getting out of bed, while showering, shaving, doing hair, dressing, or, formally, in Church.

The remainder of the day is spent doing acts of obedience (your duty well) and charity. As everyone knows, or should know, what his or her duty is—and it *is* different for each vocation and station in life—I need not go into that, other than to say: do it well, with *joy and hope.*

The actual practice of charity will depend upon your particular duty and your particular fault(s). For instance, if your duty is parent and your fault is anger, do not, in the name of charity, smile mildly at your child who pouts when you tell him to do something. Conversely, don't beat the child in a fit of anger. No. Aware of your own inadequacy, but accepting your assignment as parent from the hand of God, and controlling your own faults, discipline your child in a manner that allows him to learn and correct his ways. You must practice those acts which are required most by your state in life: as parent, discipline; as spouse, selfless and serving love; as friend, dependability; as teacher, understanding and patience; as student, humble docility; as priest, supernatural charity; as religious, community; as a creature of God, confident and joyful obedience.

Complain as little as possible of the wrongs you suffer, the weaknesses you show, the failures you bring about. It is certain that anyone who complains is engaging in self-love, self-indulgence. If injuries are real and complaint is necessary first try to remedy the offense; this not done, only complain to someone with a calm soul who loves God truly. Otherwise, instead of easing your heart, you provoke it to greater passion. To help you in these matters, look inward frequently, reflecting upon Christ Our Lord: naked, blasphemed, slandered, crucified, forsaken, overwhelmed with every kind of trouble, sorrow and labor. This inward reflection puts things into perspective: you *never* suffer anything equal to what He did and does suffer for and from you.

For this to come about, you must strip yourself of vanity. Vanity is understood to be a kind of glory which we assume to ourselves, either for that which is not in us, or for that which is in us but not of us, or for that which is in us and of us, but does not deserve glory. Things that are not in us nor of us are heritage, favor, honor, and popularity. Things that are in us and of us but do not deserve to be gloried in are physical appearance; knowledge; ability to dance, sing, play, or tell stories; our clothes; a well-trimmed beard, mustache, or curly locks; make-up, pierced ears, soft hands, or large biceps. Are those people not weak-spirited who desire to increase their worth and raise their reputation by such frivolous and foolish things; who fancy themselves learned because they have gained a little knowledge and act as if everyone should go to school to them; who picture themselves as good-looking or beautiful—and only because someone made the mistake of telling them so—and who strut around like peacocks and think themselves to be admired by everyone? All of this is extremely vain, offensive, and foolish.

At the same time, do not say you are nothing unless you mean it. A good gauge is what you would say or do if someone took you at your word and told others that you are nothing or left you because he wanted nothing to do with nothing. Do not pretend to retire or hide from the world so that the world will really run after you and seek you out. Do not feign lowliness when you really want to sit at the head table; lastness when you really desire firstness. Do not utter words of true love unless there is a sincere, interior sentiment to match the words. Do not cast your head or eyes down unless they are pulled down by a pure heart. Do not desire to be humble unless you desire it with all your heart. Do not confuse lying and shameful eyes with the eyes of a humble heart.

To imagine you know what you do not know is vanity; to say you do not know when you do is vanity. Charity requires us to instruct our brother when the opportune moment presents itself, and tell him what is profitable for his conversion and salvation. Therefore, don't pretend to be either a fool or a wise man. Charity forbids you to play the sage or the prophet and forbids you to counterfeit the fool. As sin is the opposite of love, so acting, lying, and intrigue are the opposite of honesty and sincerity.

So, if the world looks upon you as abject and a fool because you act in a manner which evidences a true love, a sincere devotion to God and His Church, an obedience to law and duty, and a patience with failure and weakness, charity will make you rejoice at this reproach. If you are mad or sad because the world accuses, abuses, and misuses you, you are egoistic. There's your yardstick to measure the charity in your heart.

H. Retreat

The last step is retreat. As our human nature falls away so easily from its proper affections, right desires, and good will on account of its frailty and the inclinations of sin, we must, for these reasons, renew and repeat the solid resolutions. By neglecting to do so, we run the very dangerous risk of relapsing into our former state.

Keep this in mind. There is no clock as there is no soul, which must not be wound up, reset, cleansed, and oiled. So, besides winding it up every day, it should be sent to be repaired once a year. The person who is truly careful with his soul will give it a thorough checkup once a year with the help of a spiritual director. Simultaneously, he will rekindle his heart and recoup his strength.

You should choose a time and a place. It should be in solitude for a period of two days, at least, under the direction of your confessor or spiritual director. The solitude should be both actual and spiritual.

The following should be met in your retreat (which means both withdrawal *and* do over).

I—Your conversion
II—Your advancement
III—Your present state or condition; how does your heart stand towards:
    1. God, His laws
    2. Church, its laws
    3. Neighbor
    4. Faith
    5. Hope
    6. Charity
    7. Duty
    8. Obedience
    9. Patience
    10. Chastity

11. Temperance
12. Decency
13. Respect
14. Rash judgment
15. Sadness
16. Slander
17. Anxiety
18. Despair
19. Lack of discipline
20. Temptations
21. Occasions to sin
22. Pastimes and recreations
23. Prayer (dryness)
24. Sacraments
25. Mass

Examine each carefully. Begin each examination with a prayer for assistance. Ask your director for a schedule. Do not go to confession until you have completed your examination. Do not hesitate to use paper and pencil to help you. Be honest—the only one you are fooling is yourself.

On the day when you finish your retreat, you should be your renewed self. You will have fixed your resolutions firm in your heart. You will return quietly, but firmly, to your ordinary and daily affairs and associations. Therefore, your resolutions must penetrate throughout all parts of your soul without effort of mind or body. Your retreat is a failure if they do not, and this means you have done something wrong.

The Start

"My brothers, be united in following my rule of life, take as your models everybody who is already doing this and study them as you used to study us. I have told you often, and I repeat it today with tears, there are many who are behaving as the enemies of the Cross of Christ. They are destined to be lost. They make fools into their god and they are proudest of something they ought to think shameful; the things they think important are earthly things. For us, our homeland is in Heaven, and from it comes the Savior we are waiting for, the Lord Jesus Christ, and he will transfigure these wretched bodies of ours into copies of his Glorious Body. He will do that by the same power with which he can subdue the whole universe. So then, my brothers and dear friends, do not give way but remain faithful in the Lord. I miss you very much, dear friends; you are my joy and my crown."

(Phil. 3:17—4:1)

The truth of what is contained in this treatise will not be popular so you must not expect more than a few men and women to be with you. Also, you must expect ridicule, criticism, and even abuse: that is always the way of truth. In spite of this you must go about quietly, diligently, unassertively, and faithful to your resolutions, leading yourself and others to the Heavenly City. You must lead yourself in a manner that is in accord with your moral and spiritual condition. People are able to receive the truths of Christ and His Church according to their own moral and spiritual disposition. Further, these Truths of God are to be approached with wonder and fear, not with the axe of a critical intellect or a desire for novelty. As I have tried to show, conversion is a principle of action, not mere intellectual assent; thus, the primacy of moral and spiritual disposition.

God wants us to do something and to do it now. This means that the best safeguard to faith is a rightly disposed will (love, as St. Paul calls it), which acts through holiness, under obedience, and in charity. God must be embraced, not examined at arm's length in a detached fashion. Even pagans caution us that true knowledge in morals can only be gained by practice: a just man becomes just by performing just acts. And St. John, in his Gospel, stresses many times the relationship of obedience to love and of love to knowledge. Acts of obedience confirm the experience of disposing the will rightly; this disposition makes prayer possible, leads to the love of God, and culminates in knowing Him. Our tendency, however, is to gain knowledge of God by any means but obedience.

That there is knowledge which is boundless and infinitely good is not denied. It is of no measure, however, if the will is not prepared for it by acts of obedience. Knowledge of good and evil, remember, along with physical death, is a fruit of that first act of human disobedience: Original Sin. So, what must prepare for the Truth is the Way: *Conversion*. Without the whole Christ, there is no going, no doing. Only if we abide in God's Way, which is obedience to His commands, will we know the Truth.

If we had been faithful to Him since Baptism, we never would need conversion. In Baptism we were all made children of God and we would have reaped the benefits: God's grace would have flowed according to our capacities, hallowing our childhood, strengthening our youth, controlling us in the perils of opening adulthood, mastering each wayward thought, subduing each rising appetite. Had we cooperated with it, it would have flowed on, peaceably and gently, through us, and we never would have needed this sharp, painful turnaround, this conversion. The Way had to be reopened to us. Therefore, we need not stand in fear and alarm but, rather, we must ask forgiveness for our trespasses and, step by step, begin the journey along the Way to the Truth and Life.

The will, cooperating with grace, and supported by prayer, begins the act-by-act, feature-by-feature change. And this change is not a marked change which is immediately apparent because the change is an ever ongoing, internal, and spiritual change. Even the weak, the frail, the wayward, the self-indulgent, and the self-willed can make this conversion because they receive a strength from grace within them that is mightier than the power of Satan and the world. The grace promised us is given, not that we can know more, but that we may be better. It is given to influence, guide, and strengthen us in performing our duty towards God and men. It is given to us as creatures, sinners. It teaches us what we are, where we are going, what we must do, and how we must do it. It enables us to change our fallen will from evil to good, to make ourselves a "new" will. And since men tend to prize knowledge above holiness, we must be warned that this enlightening is not an understanding of mysteries, but a call to obedience to, and a love for, the laws of God. All of Holy Scripture gives us but one rule, one test, one way of attaining the Truth: whether we have a loving fear of God, keep His commandments, and conform to His will. All depends upon what we do, day by day, to make ourselves less earthly and more heavenly.

It is in vain, the Sacred Book repeatedly points out, that men strive to obtain or retain their belief in things Divine, while they cleave to things of this earth. It is in vain that people aspire to higher and holy things, while their life is wrong. They will attempt to convince themselves, but it is in vain; they study but it is of no use. They will even strive to work themselves up to believe them, desire to believe them, but they cannot. As their thoughts are more and more occupied with the world, Holy Truth becomes fainter and fainter, even while they regret it and wish to retain or recover it. Soon, except for the grace of God, they cannot recall it or retrace it.

Now, They Need Conversion

Their conversion must be a journey back to God. They must be led in a persuasive, positive manner which takes into account their existing knowledge, experiences, convictions, opinions, and character. It must not be inconsistent with what they know or what they have experienced. It must not unsettle them; it must be a venture. St. Paul demanded from neither Jew nor Gentile immediate and full faith in his message: he looked them squarely in the eye, steadfastly holding their gaze, to see whether they had faith enough to be converted. He appealed to the whole realm and range of opinions, affections, and desires which made up, in each man, his moral and spiritual self, which, distinct from all random guesses and efforts, would set him forward in one steady direction. If it was what it should be, the person would respond to the Apostle's teaching as the strings of one instrument vibrate with another. If it was not, the person would neither accept nor abide in it. He taught men that Almighty God is Omnipotent *AND* that He has moral qualities: He is Just, Holy, Merciful, and True. He taught them that God already dwells within them as Lawgiver and Judge by showing them shame.

St. Paul is our example of converter and convert. Let me close with this thought.

You will be told—you will tell yourself—that this instruction is so complex, arduous, and time-consuming, that anyone who takes it seriously must do nothing else; it is impractical and impossible, particularly if you live in the world: working, family obligations, etc.

Nice try.

Please don't end this reading by beginning to lie to yourself or by buying someone else's lie.

If all that is contained here was performed every day, all day, without fail, it certainly would be our whole occupation. However, you must remember my opening comment about love as excellence within place and with others. It is necessary to perform these exercises at their proper time and in their proper place and as opportunities for them are presented. For example, how many laws exist which you are required to observe every day, all day, without fail? Is it not understood that you observe them when called upon to observe them? That you observe them at the time, place, and occasion which demands you to obey them? That the laws of traffic apply to the licensed driver only when he is driving? That the laws of Mass attendance do not apply if sickness is present?

Also, do not say that this guide is only for the few: "not for everybody." It is for anybody who wants it. *ANYBODY* can engage in this activity, even the proud and the ignorant. If this were not true, we would have to deny the universality of Christ, His message, His Church. Not everybody can do this alone: we need good guides and the will to endure whatever pains are necessary to obtain the object of our solid resolution: God and the Kingdom of Heaven.

I entreat, I implore, I plead with you to persevere in the life of true love: let everybody be ready when Judgment comes. Look up to Heaven; do not forget it while on earth. Look down into Hell; do not cast yourself into it for the sake of fleeting things. Look upon Christ—He is the "Way, the Truth, and the Life."

Let us, then, not ask God, "What can I do with my life?" But, rather, let us ask our Lord, "What must I do with my life?" When we ask "what can I do," we are indicating we may not have the commitment to follow through. But, when we ask "what must I do," we find commitment to do what God has commanded: "Love one another as I have loved you" (Jn. 15:13).

Our Father, Who is in Heaven, Who sent His only-begotten Son to redeem and sanctify each individual person, is not pleased with a half-hearted life: "...Ephraim is a cake not turned" (Hos. 7:8). This Old Testament proclamation by a passionate prophet pales before the words of Christ in the Book of Revelation: "Being what you are, lukewarm, neither cold nor hot, you will make me vomit you out of my mouth" (Rv. 3:16).

These citations from Holy Scripture, the promulgations by Holy Mother Church, and the charisms of our Papal Fathers say much about commitment to a Christian life.

If we keep in our mind the image presented by Hosea, we will be reminded constantly that the cake not turned is burned on the bottom and uncooked on the top.

Let us not be nominal Catholics. All should remember the admonition of the Apostle: "Each of us will have to give an account of himself before God" (Rom. 14:12).

Conclusion

"Let not your heart be troubled.
You believe in God: believe also in me."

(Jn. 14:1)

An essential fruit of true spiritual living is the confidence that gives sweetness to our intimacy with the person of Jesus Christ. A primary benefit of this confidence is supernatural peace: "Peace I leave with you, my peace I give unto you" (Jn. 14:27).

Whoever loses confidence has drawn back from the generous heart of Christ. Whoever is troubled has stumbled from the loving arms of the King of Peace.

"Let us love our littleness; let us love to feel nothing. Then we shall be pure in spirit and Jesus will come seeking us, however far away we are. He will transform us into flames of love" (Little Flower).

Confidence and peace—without limits!

"Have confidence, I have overcome the world" (Jn. 16:33).

Be confident and peaceful in the failures of spiritual life, in the failures of everyday life. We may lose everything, but we do not have the right to lose our confidence and peace. Further, it is a duty for us to spread this hopeful confidence and joyous peace —they should radiate from our face. Jesus expects to find them in the hearts of us, His friends, and that they be shown to our friends. Generosity!

Of course, when we see ourselves to be so unworthy, so fainthearted, falling every moment, how could we not be tempted against this confidence and peace? Because we believe too much in our own wretchedness and not enough in merciful love, the question always arises: "Is the love of Jesus, His merciful love, *really* so great; is it as great as that?"

Don't fall into this trap.

His love *is* without limits; His mercy *is* infinite. Yes, He does love us immensely, to the utmost limit: "He loved them unto the end" (Jn. 13:1).

Again, the Little Flower tells us:

"I am not always faithful, but I never get discouraged. I abandon myself into the arms of Jesus and there I find again all that I have lost and much more besides."

Now do we understand "empty hands"?

We have nothing, He has everything. He wants to fill our empty hands with the limitless gifts of His love. This is the basis of the interior life, the foundation of the spiritual life, the purpose of redemption, the reason for the Holy Eucharist.

We find unsuspected joy and hope in the reality of "empty hands" because we do not notice our pain, heed our fatigue or feel sorry for ourself. What is more, we have the happiness of speaking about Christ, of opening the clenched fists of others into empty hands. We taste the joy of spreading joy, the hope of giving hope, the peace of bringing peace.

All of this is nothing but the Gospel, and the Gospel is for everyone. It is neither a theory nor a theological demonstration. It is a way of life.

> "As the Father has loved me, I also have loved you. Abide in my love.... These things I have spoken to you that my joy may be in you, and your joy may be filled. This is my commandment, that you love one another, as I have loved you.... You are my friends...because all things whatsoever I have heard from my Father, I have made known to you. You have not chosen me, but I have chosen you" (Jn. 15:9, 11, 15, 16).

Acknowledgments

In Part One, the purpose of using numerous images and many real-life examples is to move media-oriented people toward serious interior reflection and to prepare them gradually for the directives found in Part Two. The choice to use this approach is mine. Some of the method and many of the materials have come from the pamphlets of the Christophers, to whom this writer is indebted.

The interweaving of many writers, speakers and thinkers in Part Two is also my choice and I acknowledge readily that this section is theirs and not mine.

My deep gratitude is extended to Mother Paula, D.S.P., for her generosity; Sr. Concetta, D.S.P., for her persistence; and Cynthia Nicolosi, a student at Magdalen College, for her perseverance. Finally, the paternal guidance of H. Lyman Stebbins and Fr. Cyril Karam, O.S.B., directed this author toward tenderness.

J.D.M.

Daughters of St. Paul

MASSACHUSETTS
50 St. Paul's Ave., Jamaica Plain, Boston, MA 02130; **617-522-8911.**
172 Tremont Street, Boston, MA 02111; **617-426-5464; 617-426-4230.**
NEW YORK
78 Fort Place, Staten Island, NY 10301; **212-447-5071; 212-447-5086.**
59 East 43rd Street, New York, NY 10017; **212-986-7580.**
625 East 187th Street, Bronx, NY 10458; **212-584-0440.**
525 Main Street, Buffalo, NY 14203; **716-847-6044.**
NEW JERSEY
Hudson Mall—Route 440 and Communipaw Ave.,
Jersey City, NJ 07304; **201-433-7740.**
CONNECTICUT
202 Fairfield Ave., Bridgeport, CT 06604; **203-335-9913.**
OHIO
2105 Ontario Street (at Prospect Ave.), Cleveland, OH 44115;
216-621-9427.
616 Walnut Street, Cincinnati, OH 45202; **513-421-5733; 513-721-5059.**
PENNSYLVANIA
1719 Chestnut Street, Philadelphia, PA 19103; **215-568-2638;
215-864-0991.**
VIRGINIA
1025 King Street, Alexandria, VA 22314; **703-683-1741; 703-549-3806.**
SOUTH CAROLINA
243 King Street, Charleston, SC 29401.
FLORIDA
2700 Biscayne Blvd., Miami, FL 33137; **305-573-1618; 305-573-1624.**
LOUISIANA
4403 Veterans Memorial Blvd., Metairie, LA 70006; **504-887-7631;
504-887-0113.**
423 Main Street, Baton Rouge, LA 70802; **504-343-4057; 504-381-9485.**
MISSOURI
1001 Pine Street (at North 10th), St. Louis, MO 63101; **314-621-0346;
314-231-1034.**
ILLINOIS
172 North Michigan Ave., Chicago, IL 60601; **312-346-4228; 312-346-3240.**
TEXAS
114 Main Plaza, San Antonio, TX 78205; **512-224-8101; 512-224-0938.**
CALIFORNIA
1570 Fifth Ave., San Diego, CA 92101; **619-232-1442.**
46 Geary Street, San Francisco, CA 94108; **415-781-5180.**
WASHINGTON
2301 Second Ave., Seattle, WA 98121; **206-623-1320; 206-623-2234.**
HAWAII
1143 Bishop Street, Honolulu, HI 96813; **808-521-2731.**
ALASKA
750 West 5th Ave., Anchorage, AK 99501; **907-272-8183.**

CANADA
3022 Dufferin Street, Toronto 395, Ontario, Canada.